ASTROLOGY
AND
PSYCHOANALYSIS

Understanding Astrology Through the Lens of Freudian Psychology

By
Clifford West

Table of Contents

The expressions in life which occur around us appear in multitudes too numerous to contemplate yet, they are ultimately a cast of few. If we know those few, we will know them all. The most complex of behavior and circumstance boils down to some very simple principles.

1

Introduction

For thousands of years, diverse cultures throughout the world have taken note of the astronomical bodies that move through the sky in patterned regularity. Ultimately, the complex and varied cycles of the Sun, Moon and planets had come to embody symbolic principles to different cultures in different times. As seasons changed and qualitative transformations occurred in the passing of time, philosophical speculation lead some to view the processes on the Earth and the universe above to be in sympathetic accord. The premise "as above, so below" came to define the belief that astronomical bodies and events indeed symbolized events and personality types existing in the world.

In recent decades the age-old "science" of astrology (considered "superstition" by many), has experienced a rebirth. Books on astrology can now be found that have been written by psychologists who see astrology as a valid construct in which to view psychological processes. Most of these inquiries express a distinct bias for the "Jungian" school of psychology, thus viewing planets and signs as archetypal symbols representing basic universal patterns. Although Jungian principles easily lend themselves to esoteric perspectives, astrological symbolism needn't be confined to this one school of psychological thought.

Jung's mentor, Sigmund Freud, though rigidly rejecting mystic-occult perspectives, outlined in his theories on psychoanalysis the basic drives and restraining mechanisms at work within the human psyche. These processes, though given different names, are the same processes that astrology addresses in its metaphorical view of human behavior and motivation. Astrology is ultimately a valid construct in which to view psychoanalytic processes.

2

Freud and Psychoanalytic Processes

The foundation of Freud's theories initially rested upon his belief in what he called *the pleasure principle*, the concept whereby humans are motivated to seek pleasure and avoid pain. He saw this hunger-like drive within humans as specifically sexual in nature and referred to it as libido. This instinctual energy was inevitably seen to confront an outer world which demanded restraint from pervasive indulgence. Freud referred to these prohibitions within society as *the reality principle.*

Freud eventually clarified the relationship between the conflicting "Pleasure" and "Reality" principles in his description of *the Id, Ego, and Superego*. In this system of appraisal, the mind was ultimately seen to consist of three distinct functions acting at various levels of consciousness or unconsciousness. Within these concepts lay the individual's drive for pleasure and the personal and interjected societal restraints to that expression.

In later years Freud had modified his theories to incorporate the concept of *Thanatos,* or death instinct. Thanatos was seen as a drive to reduce tension to the ultimate state of inertia.

Few academic-minded individuals would likely see Freud's psychoanalytic concepts in the symbolism of astrology, however, when we examine the traditional meanings of *planets, signs,* and the *houses* in a horoscope, we indeed find the same processes of drives and inhibitions, consciousness, and unconsciousness.

3

The Astrological Vocabulary

How it "Works"

Astrology is a concept that often has to be defended when confronted with a skeptical audience. Many books on the subject seek to justify it as an operation of gravity, radiation, or some other yet unknown power that "influences." This writer has not found astrological correlations with personality and circumstance to be a result of *cause and effect*. Indeed, an astrology chart is not really constructed for a person per se but, more specifically, for a given time or place. Whatever begins in that time and place seems to get caught up in the symbolic qualities of that moment or location and its course of existence unfolds from that point of departure ("birth") - be it a baby, a marriage, or business. Abstract institutions like marriage are not likely to be effected by physical influences like gravity. An astrologer believes that conceptual entities prosper, falter, or develop, like people, in accordance with the placement and movement of astronomical positions — a *synchronicity* or "meaningful coincidence." In essence everything has a "personality." The universe (at least *our* universe) manifests with a recipe of some very basic symbolic ingredients.

Basic archetypal concepts like aggressiveness /passiveness, the enduring/ the transitory, substantive/elusive etc. all replicate on infinite fractal-like levels in nature, human personality, and cultural constructs. "Mother" is qualitatively different than "father" just as the Sun is intrinsically different than the Moon both in appearance and essence. The recurring attributes and events of existence repeat and mutate like a qualitative echo that defines existence. Just as a good poetic description can capture the essence of a person or thing, an astrological description can work in much the same way.

The Language of Astrology

The astrological vocabulary consists of descriptive meanings attached to the astronomical bodies and their relative position to each other and sectioned reference points in the sky. The unique configurations formed at a given time are believed by an astrologer to coincide with the qualities of an entity as it emerges independently at a point in time and space. The ultimate result of such a "map" — *horoscope* — is a description of the unique energy expression of drives and restraints in an individual — a psychological profile.

A detailed discussion of how an astrological chart is constructed and what all planets and signs symbolize is beyond the scope of this brief inquiry. In understanding the "basics" of astrology however, one must understand that planets (for descriptive ease the Sun and Moon are included as "planets") represent active processes. The twelve signs that the planets move through over time are ways in which these processes are expressed. In essence, planets are "verbs" in the astrological vocabulary; the signs, as modifying influences, are "adverbs". The houses are where the action takes place (i.e. domestically, publicly, with a partner, etc.). These principles (planets, signs, and houses) share relationships with one another. For example, Mars is said to "rule" Aries, meaning Mars is the action principle of the Aries concept. The complex combinations which occur at a given point in time are observed by an astrologer to discern subtleties of character far beyond the "sun sign" readings of popular culture. The specific meaning of each planet, sign, and house can be seen to correlate to basic principles in human psychology, thus it is no coincidence that this ancient system and Freud's psychoanalysis often describe similar processes.

The Astrological Horoscope — esoteric map of the human psyche

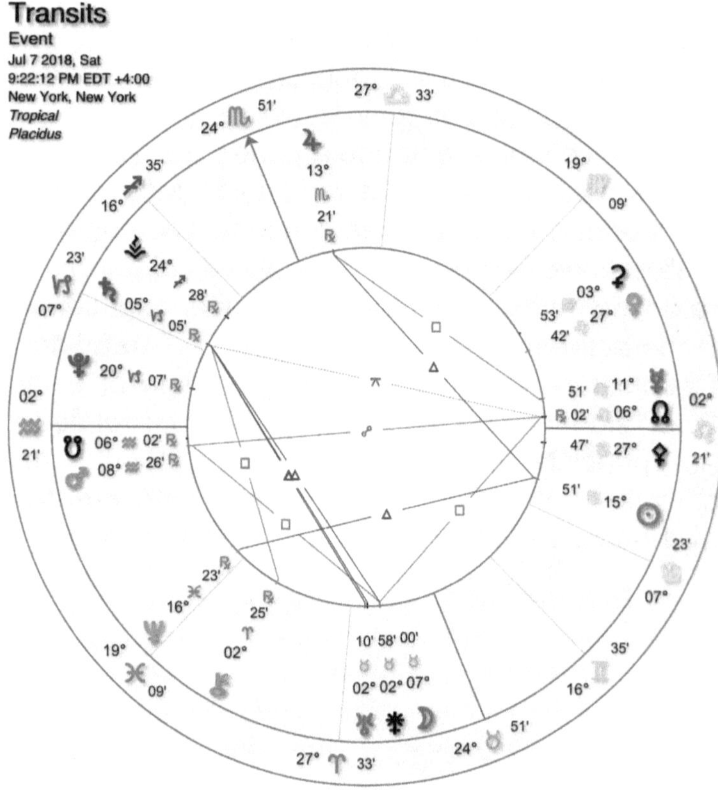

4

Mars — the Id / Sex, and Aggression

The planet Mars in astrology has traditionally been associated with sex and aggression. More recently science has come to see physiological correlation between these concepts. (Greene, Dynamics, 4) The aggressive and sexually-oriented nature of Mars' symbolism is akin to Freud's concept of the Id. Its nature is instinctual, primitive, and unrestrained, an aggressive force of ". . . blind impulse to self-affirmation, to the expression of all elements of one's being, without any discrimination of choice, without any concern for consequences, without any concern for others." (Greene, Dynamics, 8)

In an individual horoscope, when Mars is prominently placed and unrestrained by other factors, the person is expected to be noticeably aggressive, impulsive, and selfishly child-like. Such manifestations of the pleasure principle and unconscious drives for satiation are inevitably confronted with the *reality principle* (reality!) and the restrictive attributes of *Ego and Superego.*

5

The Sun, Moon, and Saturn — Ego and Superego / Rules, Guilt, Restriction, and Blockage

In the astrological context, Sigmund Freud's concepts of Ego and Superego are defined by the interactions between the sun, moon, and Saturn. The sun, as the conscious aspect of the ego, defines the development of ego-identity as the Id attempts to reconcile itself with external reality. The moon, as an unconscious polarity to the sun, is akin to that part of the Ego which remains submerged beneath consciousness and thus interacts closely with the Id. As an instrument of emotions and sensitivity, it registers anxiety associated with forbidden impulses in childhood. At this point the planet Saturn, as symbol of the Superego, comes to intervene for society's social and moral standards. Rules, guilt, restriction, and all manner of "blockage" act under the designs of the so-called "lord of Karma". (Arroyo 9) Whether one uses such mystical allusions or not, Saturn in the horoscope is ultimately the supreme symbol of the reality principle.

"In traditional astrology Saturn is known as a malefic planet. Even his virtues are rather dreary — self-control, tact, thrift, caution-

-and his vices are particularly unpleasant because they operate through the emotion we call fear. . . He is usually considered to be the bringer of limitation, frustration, hard work, and self-denial, and even his bright side is usually associated with wisdom and self-discipline . . . he is the dweller at the threshold, the keeper of the keys to the gate . . ." (Greene, Saturn, 10-11)

Saturn and the Superego both represent interjected parental authority. Saturn and its related sign Capricorn represent the principle in human psychic life that is inhibitory and paradoxically achievement-oriented (as a sublimated response to frustration). Though not all "Capricorns" (in popular "Sun Sign" astrology) are expected to necessarily adhere to such stereotyped behavior, those individuals with this sign or the planet Saturn prominent in their birth charts are found to exhibit noticeable *saturnine* traits. When libido/id energy is blocked (Saturn) excessively, the trade-off is inevitably power and ambition. Such sublimation of libido energy is characteristic of Saturn aspects (angular positions) to the moon, or the moon in the sign Capricorn. Understanding the symbolism of the moon and its role in Ego sensitivity to childhood impulse anxieties, one can see the combination of Saturn-Moon as the Superego and Ego's role in repression.

Not all "Moon in Capricorn" individuals will be necessarily ruthless in their ambitions, but one need only compare this astrological/psychoanalytic trait to those famous personalities who shared it as examples of sublimated repression: Adolf Hitler, Napoleon Bonaparte, Otto Von Bismarch, General George Patton. (Erlewine 89-19-46-83) In Adolf Hitler's horoscope one also finds the planet Saturn prominent (at the highest point in the chart) and "squaring" (the 90-degree angle particularly indicative of blockage) the planet Mars. (Green, The Outer Planet, 56)

Intense inner frustration and a feeling of weakness and powerlessness are two of the more difficult side-effects of Mars-Saturn contacts [repression of libido], and it often becomes necessary for the individual to impose his will on others in a forceful way. . . .

> There appears to be some connection with the parents here, as with all Saturn contacts, and the key to many of the Mars-Saturn behavior patterns lies in the individual's childhood. . . . There is often a stifling or punishment of early sexual curiosity. (Greene, Saturn, 118)

An element of repression even greater than that of the planet Saturn is found in the symbolism of the planet Pluto and the sign Scorpio.

6

Pluto — Repression and Catharsis / Depth, Darkness, and Intensity

The planet Pluto, discovered in the 1930's, came to be seen as behaving in association with the astrological sign Scorpio. Both concepts are seen by astrologers to embody qualities of obsession, fixation, and catharsis, as well as relating to the various defense mechanisms which allow "reduction of tension by means of denying reality, falsifying it or distorting it." (Niemann 160), like the symbolism of a blocked volcano needing to erupt, Pluto

> brings to the surface that which must be eliminated. This same Plutonian force began to be active on a larger scale at the same time Pluto was discovered, as seen in the Freudian approach to psychology (bringing to light all 'repressed' psychic material) and in the rise of Nazism (bringing to the surface the unsuspected demons that lurk beneath the facade of 'civilization'). Transits [the predictive aspects of astrology indicating changing astrological principles through time] of Pluto have a similar influence, bringing to the surface that which is ready for elimination and destruction.(Arroyo, 54)

The symbolism of Pluto, as a description of tension build-up and release, can also be seen along with Mars as a specific astrological indicator of sexuality. As a concept relating to death and rebirth (specifically, "transformation"), there is some affinity to Freud's concept of *Thanatos* (the "death wish") as well. Curiously, the sex act itself is often called "the little death" in french (Idemon, audio tape). Sex, the "death instinct," and defense mechanisms all seek to eliminate tension, a process described by astrology's Pluto-Scorpio and Freud's psychoanalysis. Beyond these principles we also find Pluto-Scorpio symbolism to relate to taboos and thus they are appropriate metaphors for the very concepts of psychoanalysis — probing with ruthless honesty into the deep and secret, and hidden.

> "In all aspects involving Pluto . . . the individual feels the pressure to confront a certain taboo. . . . The first impulse in most people is to try to control this tendency by repression. However, many people eventually find that this pent-up transformative power impels them to confront the taboos and to break through their restrictions. . . . The taboos must be confronted since all the psychic garbage, fears, attachments, and negativity have to be brought to the surface in order to be outgrown or transmuted." (Arroyo 68)

Pluto-Scorpio's affinity to repression and release

can also be seen as descriptive of the concepts of power and control. These qualities particularly suit it further in describing Freud's "Anal" stage of psycho-sexual development. Together with Saturn-Capricorn, a powerfully placed Pluto-Scorpio in the birth chart is often indicative of the "anal-retentive" temperament, where one has learned to control, manipulate, and express a sense of power, beginning with early experiences in toilet training. (Niemann 163-164)

One can observe many of the previously described "Pluto" issues in the expressions of those whose astrological chart features a prominent Pluto: the very "Plutonian" philosopher, Friedrich Nietzsche and his "will to power", William Peter Blatty, the author of, "The Exorcist," surreal film director, David Lynch, and cult leader, Charles Manson, to name a few. (Erlewine 47) If one views such characteristics beyond mere descriptions of human temperament, then it is interesting to note that a chart done for the time and place of Lenin's taking power in Russia produces a "Sun in Scorpio, squaring Saturn" in the "personality" of the former Soviet Union. (Greene, The Outer Planets 116) It is equally noteworthy that Freud himself had the Scorpio-Pluto concepts prominent in his astrological chart. (Greene, The Outer Planets 70)

7

Neptune — the Unconscious / Dreams, Escapism, and Transcendence

Beyond the previously described astrological determiners of unconscious factors in a personality, one must address the unconscious in its most hidden and diffuse form.

The sign Pisces and the planet Neptune are often correlated with Carl Jung's "collective unconscious." It is in the symbolism of these astrological indicators that one finds ego boundaries dissolved to the point where one's identity is ultimately with the infinite. By identifying with the infinite, the individual is paradoxically weak and amorphous yet omnipotent, by virtue of their lack of ego boundaries. It is the Neptunian personality who paradoxically states that god is everywhere and "I am God." As a manifestation of this sense of transcendence, such an individual may "lose themselves" in drugs, alcohol, fantasy, or psychosis, or elevate themselves into the timeless realms of spiritual clarity. Either way an individual in such a state can be seen to be manifesting the qualities Freud described in his commentaries on narcissism. (Niemann 158) It isn't just the brash and arrogant who are narcissists but often those who feign humility the most.

———

8

———

The Outer Planets and Examples of Development Through Time

Overly prominent outer planets (or their respective signs) in an astrological chart are often indicative of some of the traits Freud described as *neurotic*. Today, some may see them as exhibiting characteristics seen as being "on the autism spectrum." While it's debatable as to what exactly this means for the individual in question, it does tend to set them apart from more mundane values and behavior. The very attributes that may appear "weird" or eccentric to others are often the very traits that exhibit creativity and the ability to think — and live — outside of the box.

Libidinal energy that is frustrated or repressed and ego identity that is transcended is characteristic of the qualities symbolized by particular astrological markers. These same concepts can be seen to emerge or develop over time as well, beyond the static embodiment in a birth chart.

So-called "transits", in astrological jargon, refer to the motion of planets at a given time in reference to the original locations in one's birth chart. Characteristically, Saturn still acts in its role as symbol of blockage (frustration).

An interesting example can be seen in the astrological chart of former president Richard Nixon. At birth, the sun in his chart (the conscious Ego) was in the middle of the sign Capricorn (already a strong Saturnine quality). A chart done for July 4, 1776 (the "birth" of the United States as a political entity) places the Sun in the middle of the sign Cancer (significantly the point across from Richard Nixon's sun). When the former president left the White House to avoid threat of impeachment, the planet Saturn at that specific time was in the middle of Cancer, said to be "conjunct" the U.S. chart's sun and opposite Richard Nixon's chart's sun. (Lewi,74)

Pluto can be seen to behave in similar ways in transit. In keeping with its symbolism, astrologically and in reference to psychoanalysis, Pluto dredges up psychic toxins; it is catharsis and transformation. Although it ultimately frees up repressed energies, the process usually parallels a period of painful emotional upheaval and often coincides with some type of psychotherapy. (Idemon, audio tape) Interestingly, one can again see the concept in action in relation to a country. As was stated earlier, a chart for the former Soviet Union places the sun in Scorpio (already a strong "plutonion" influence). Specifically, the sun was in the middle of Scorpio. Pluto takes the better part of 250 years to travel around the sun and through the signs (and therefore through a chart). From 1988 to 1990 Pluto was "transiting" in the middle of Scorpio, "conjunct" the Soviet Union's sun. (Green, The Outer Planets, 119-120)

The astrological principles had acted, as they would in an individual's chart, in accord with the Freudian concept of catharsis (in this case the upheaval and complete implosion of the Soviet Union as a coherent entity).

———

9

———

Qualities in Harmony and Discord

Another multi-dimensional aspect in astrology can be seen in the interactions between two or more charts. Called <I>synastry,</I> the concept of comparing charts sees the same psychological factors which occur in individual horoscopes as interacting between different horoscopes as well. Oftentimes factors in another's chart (personality) exacerbate problems or enhance the strengths innate in one's own birth chart.

> "Often the reaction on a conscious level to a close Saturn contact [between charts] is a dislike or animosity of a particularly irrational kind. This is good testimony to the maxim that we hate or fear within others, what we find within ourselves. Equally often the characteristic Saturnian phenomenon of overcompensation is displayed, and the person experiences a kind of compulsive fascination toward his 'attacker'--and prepares himself, unconsciously, for the eventual conquering and disarming of his foe. This, frighteningly enough, is often called love." (Green, Saturn, 150-151)

Where Saturn was seen earlier to frustrate libido (Mars) in an individual chart, one can also find a specific person's Saturn as an external source of frustration to one's own search for gratification. Likewise one can interact with a person who becomes a specific catalyst to catharsis (i.e. a psychoanalyst).

10

Conclusion

Whether viewing astrology in relation to an individual person or institution, or seeing it in context to the events which take place over time or between entities, it can be viewed as a valid template for psychological processes. Because its subject is ultimately the processes which take place within the psyche, it is no coincidence that it shares interest in the same issues that motivate modern psychological study.

In developing the meaning behind such terms as Mars, Saturn, or Pluto, astrology has covered the same insightful terrain as Sigmund Freud in probing processes in the human condition. Astrology is ultimately a valid construct in which to view Freud's psychoanalytic processes and the human psyche.

BIBLIOGRAPHY

Arroyo, Stephen. Astrology, Karma, and Transformation.
Sebastopol, Calif.: CRCS Publications, 1978.

Erlewine, Stephen, ed. The Circle Book of Charts.
Tempe, Ariz.: American Federation of Astrologers, Inc., 1982.

Greene, Liz and Howard Sasportas. Dynamics of the Unconscious.
York Beach, Maine: Samuel Weiser, Inc., 1988.

Greene, Liz. Saturn, a New Look at an Old Devil.
York Beach, Maine: Samuel Weiser, Inc. 1976.

___________. The Outer Planets and their Cycles.
Reno, Nev.: CRCS Publications, 1983.

Idemon, Richard. The Serpent and the Garden (the Scorpio-Taurus Polarity).
Audio tape, San Anselmo, Calif.: Pegasus Tapes, 1986.

Lewi, Grant. Astrology for the Millions.
St. Paul, Minn.: Llewellyn Publications, 1990.

Niemann, Henry and Judith Cooper. Astrology-Psychology.
Tempe, Ariz.: American Federation of Astrologers, Inc., 1986.

Strachey, James, ed. Sigmund Freud's Beyond the Pleasure Principle.
New York, N.Y.: W. W. Norton & Co., 1961.

__________. Sigmund Freud's Introductory Lectures on Psycho-analysis.
New York, N.Y.: W. W. Norton & Co., 1966.